21st-CENTURY SPACESHIPS

Enslow Publishing

Published in 2019 by Enslow Publishing, LLC.
101 W. 23rd Street, Suite 240, New York, NY 10011

Library of Congress Cataloging-in-Publication Data

Names: Adams, Gloria G., author.
Title: 21st century spaceships / Gloria G. Adams.
Description: New York : Enslow Publishing, LLC., 2019. | Series: Feats of 21st
    century engineering | Audience: Grades 3-6. | Includes bibliographical
    references and index.
Identifiers: LCCN 2017048845| ISBN 9780766097063 (library bound) |
    ISBN 9780766097070 (pbk.)
Subjects: LCSH: Space vehicles—Juvenile literature. | Space ships—Juvenile
    literature. | Space shuttles—Juvenile literature. | Engineering—Juvenile
    literature. | CYAC: Space vehicles. | Space ships. | Space shuttles. Engineering.
Classification: LCC TL795 .A365 2019 | DDC 629.47—dc23
LC record available at https://lccn.loc.gov/2017048845

Printed in the United States of America

To Our Readers: We have done our best to make sure all website addresses in this
book were active and appropriate when we went to press. However, the author
and the publisher have no control over and assume no liability for the material
available on those websites or on any websites they may link to. Any comments or
suggestions can be sent by e-mail to cu stomerservice@enslow.com.

Photo Credits: Cover, p. 1 (technical drawing) pluie_r/Shutterstock.com; cover,
p. 1 (space shuttle and space station) 3Dsculptor/Shutterstock.com; p. 4 Bettmann/
Getty Images; p. 8 Heritage Images/Hulton Archive/Getty Images; p. 10 Hulton
Archive/Getty Images; pp. 12-13 NASA/Getty Images; p. 15 Anadolu Agency/
Getty Images; p. 17 Science & Society Picture Library/Getty Images; p. 19
Fotograferen.net/Alamy Stock Photo; p. 23 © AP Images; p. 25 Irina Dmitrienko/
Alamy Stock Photo; p. 27 NASA Photo/Alamy Stock Photo; p. 30 Blue Origin/
Alamy Stock Photo; pp. 32, 34 Joe Raedle/Getty Images; pp. 38-39 Universal
Images Group/Getty Images; p. 40 Xinhua/Alamy Stock Photo.

CONTENTS

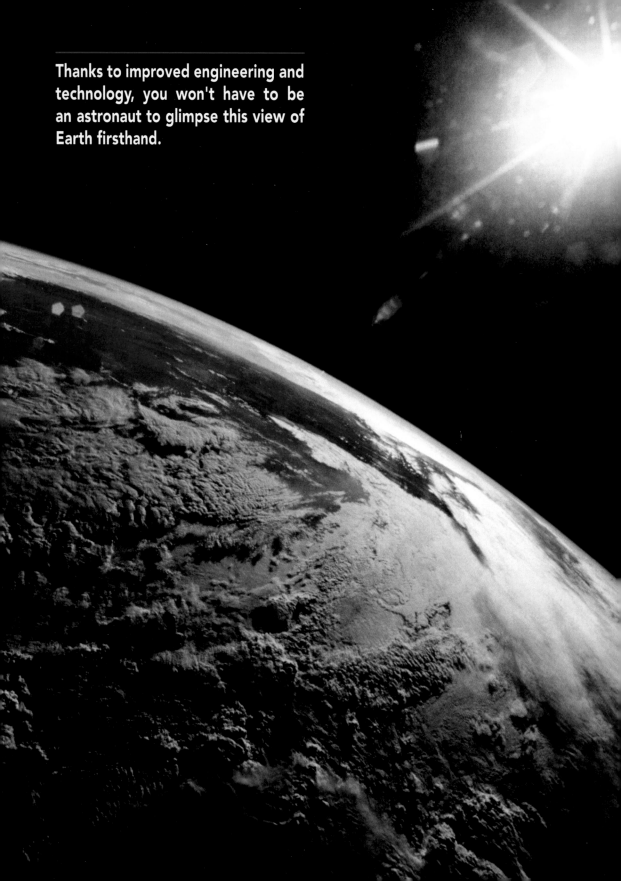

Thanks to improved engineering and technology, you won't have to be an astronaut to glimpse this view of Earth firsthand.

Introduction

What would it be like to blast off in a rocket ship and zoom through the stars in a spaceship? People have dreamed about it. Artists have painted fantastic pictures of what they think it would be like. Writers have given us stories and films that have stretched our imaginations to extremes.

Beginning in the middle of the twentieth century, some of those dreams came true. Scientists successfully launched satellites, rockets, and manned spacecraft out beyond Earth's gravity and even to the moon. They sent probes to learn about the planets of our solar system and beyond. They hoped our future would be one in which humans will travel to and live on other planets. But dreams must be based in reality.

Enter the engineers.

They are now, and always have been, the backbone of the quest for space travel. It is up to them to design and create spaceships and deal with all the very real problems of space travel. What kinds of fuel will it take and where will they store it? How can engineers make the ships lighter? How will they make them go faster? How can spaceships and any astronauts or passengers be protected from the radiation and extreme temperatures in space?

What about the danger from orbiting satellites or meteorites? How will they make room for cargo and travelers? What will they need for life-support systems? How will ships be able to land on another planet? How will they get back to Earth?

Finding the answers to these questions is the job of the engineers who work in the space science field. Many are designing ships to travel between Earth and the International Space Station (ISS). Others work on spacecraft that will travel beyond our solar system. Some design systems for fuel that will propel ships through space.

The challenges they face must be met by following the basic principles of engineering. First, a problem has to be defined. Then it has to be understood. Engineers then search for many different solutions. Those have to be tested. Finally, they need to decide which solutions will work the best.

Many hurdles have been overcome since the early days of the space age, when manned space flight was still only a fantasy. Engineers have designed satellites, probes, land rovers, and rocket ships. Even the International Space Station was designed and put together piece by piece in space. The research on that station will help scientists learn what they will need for the spaceships of tomorrow.

Plans for expeditions to Mars are underway. New ships destined to further explore the moon have been designed. Each accomplishment adds to the learning process. Because of that, scientists and engineers learn what they will need to take the next steps into the future.

This book highlights some of those accomplishments, both past and present. It shows how far engineers have come in designing today's spaceships. It also asks this question: what fantastic spaceships are in store for the future?

From Rockets to Starships

Even though space engineering has not been around for very long, it has produced some amazing engineering feats in a very short time. And it all began with rockets.

Rockets are not new inventions. They've been around for hundreds of years. For the most part, they were used as weapons. But in the early decades of the twentieth century, scientists began to experiment with rockets as the way to launch astronauts out of Earth's gravity and in to space.

Beginnings: The Space Age

Robert Goddard is often considered to be the father of modern rocketry. In 1926, he mixed gasoline with liquid oxygen to make the first liquid-propellant rocket engine. Then, in 1942, an engineer named Werner von Braun successfully launched a V2 rocket 57 miles (92 kilometers) into space. One of his colleagues said it was the day the spaceship was born.

In the late 1950s, the United States and Russia raced to put the first man into space. Russia won, but only by a few weeks. Yuri Gagarin, a Russian cosmonaut, was the first man to go into space

Yuri Gagarin, a Russian cosmonaut, was the first man to travel into space. His spaceship, *Vostok 1*, blasted off on April 12, 1961, and orbited the Earth for 108 minutes.

on April 12, 1961. The United States successfully launched astronaut Alan Shepherd into space on May 5, just twenty-three days later. The invention of the Mercury capsule made history with John Glenn, who became the first man to orbit Earth in 1962.

But the race heated up even more as Russia and the United States made plans to put a man on the moon. It would mean not only leaving the surface of Earth, but also leaving Earth's orbit. It would require a different kind of design, not only for fuel capacity and power, but also for a manned capsule and a roving lunar module to travel on the moon's surface. It would also need a way to return the astronauts to Earth. This time, the United States won the race.

In July 1969, the first manned spacecraft, *Apollo 11*, landed on the moon. It made history with Neil Armstrong's walk on the moon's surface and brought all three astronauts safely back home. Seventeen Apollo missions followed between 1969 and 1972.

But the cost for fuel and spaceships was high. Every time another spacecraft was launched, the rockets fell back into Earth's atmosphere and burned up. Upon reentry, all components except the command modules were also destroyed in the atmosphere. What was needed was a spaceship that could be used more than once. As head of manned spaceflight for the National Aeronautics and Space Administration (NASA), George Mueller had long advocated for the development of such a reusable craft. He is often credited with being the father of the space shuttle.

The space shuttle would not only fly into orbit, it would return to Earth and land like an airplane on a runway. It could also be reused for future flights.

Engineer Maxime Faget, along with many other NASA engineers, contributed years of work to the space shuttle's development. It was finally launched in 1981. During its thirty-year history, a fleet of five different space shuttles flew a total of 135 missions. The last space shuttle was retired in 2011.

During the same time, Russia developed a spacecraft named *Soyuz*. It was also designed to carry crews and cargo into space. It is still in use.

For many years, Russia and the United States were competitive. But then they began working together, along with agencies from fifteen other countries, to build and man the International Space

The first launch of NASA's space shuttle took place on April 12, 1981. The clouds of steam created at liftoff were so powerful that people had to stay at least 3 miles (4.8 km) away from the launch pad.

Station. The ISS took thirteen years to build. In 1998, the first section of the ISS went into space. By the end of the twentieth century, the ISS was ready for its first crew.

Blast Off: The Twenty-first Century

In the very first year of the twenty-first century, astronauts William Shepherd, Sergei Krikalev, and Yuri Gidzenko stepped into the new ISS. It would become a center for research, including the effects of space flight on human beings. The findings would help engineers learn what was needed to design future spaceships.

American astronauts used the space shuttle to travel to the ISS until its retirement in 2011. Then, they joined the Soviet astronauts and used their shuttle, *Soyuz*, to go to the International Space Station.

Several private companies have started their own spacecraft-development projects. In 2012, SpaceX became the first private company to use its new *Dragon* spaceship to deliver cargo to the International Space Station. *Dragon* is also designed to take a crew into space.

◦—•••→ # Exploring Mars

Before making plans to travel to Mars, scientists knew that the Red Planet, as Mars is called, had to be explored. Beginning in 1976, two American space probes, *Viking 1* and *Viking 2*, landed on Mars. Two other probes and a robotic rover called *Sojourner* followed in 1996 and 1997. Then, in 2004, two land rovers, *Spirit* and *Opportunity*, landed on Mars. *Curiosity* followed in 2012. All of the information gathered by these probes and rovers has helped engineers learn what kinds of spaceships and equipment they will need for the first manned expeditions to Mars.

The International Space Station is the largest manned object that humans have put into space. Weighing in at almost one million pounds, it travels 248 miles (400 km) above Earth, completing a global orbit in just ninety minutes.

Meanwhile, other engineers are working on plans to go to Mars. NASA is testing its newest ship, *Orion*, for expeditions. It will first travel to the moon and then to Mars.

New heavy-duty launch systems and new technologies are being developed. Harold White, a physicist at NASA, is even working on an idea for a *Star Trek*–like warp-drive engine. But until then, spaceships will not be able to travel fast enough to reach other solar systems in a reasonable amount of time. At the speeds that spaceships can currently travel, it would take thousands of years to reach the nearest star system.

One of America's probes, *Voyager 1*, has left our solar system and headed out into interstellar space. But a true starship, one that will carry astronauts or passengers to other star systems, is still a long way from becoming reality. Not until engineers can find a way to increase the speed of spaceships or discover a way to place human beings into suspended animation for extremely long voyages, will manned space travel beyond our solar system finally become possible.

Forces, Fuel, and Fire

Before humans could ever think about traveling into space, engineers had to discover how a rocket or spaceship would lift off the ground, what kind of fuel it would need, and how it would be able to return to Earth.

Takeoff

The first major obstacle to conquer was gravity. Gravity is the force that pulls us toward the center of Earth so that we don't float away. For a rocket to launch off the planet, it must have enough power to escape Earth's gravity. To manage that, it needs two things: thrust and speed.

Thrust is based on Sir Isaac Newton's principle that "to every action there is an equal and opposite reaction." For example, if you blow up a balloon, then let it go, the air will shoot out toward you and push the balloon in the opposite direction. That's how a rocket engine works. As the fuel burns up inside the rocket, it turns into a gas that pushes out toward Earth, which thrusts the rocket up into the air.

It takes both thrust and speed to lift a spacecraft off the ground and launch it high enough to escape Earth's gravitational pull.

Escape velocity is the speed that a spacecraft needs to escape Earth's gravitational pull. It needs to be faster than 25,000 miles per hour (40,233 km per hour).

Weight is another problem. The heavier the rocket, the more thrust and speed it needs to lift off. For example, at its launch site, the space shuttle had one huge external tank, two solid rocket boosters, and the shuttle itself. Altogether, when the tanks were filled with fuel, they weighed 4.4 million pounds (1.99 million kilograms). That's about the same weight as fifty eighteen-wheeler trucks!

To reach beyond Earth's atmosphere, an object must fly beyond a height of 62 miles (100 km) above sea level, an imaginary boundary that has been named the Karman Line. This is where a vehicle changes from an "aircraft" into a "spacecraft." It would take about an hour to drive that far in an automobile, but it took the space shuttle only about two and a half minutes.

Once a spaceship has passed the Karman Line, it can go into orbit. Going into orbit is like playing tug-of-war.

Gravity pulls the spaceship back toward Earth, while the speed of the ship pulls it away. For orbit to happen, the speed of the rocket or satellite must be balanced with Earth's gravitational pull. Once they are in balance, the object must maintain a speed that is just slightly less than the escape velocity.

So, engineers have managed to conquer gravity through thrust and speed. They've figured out how to keep spacecraft in orbit. What are they researching to make both takeoff and orbit even better?

One solution is called an air-breathing rocket engine. British engineer Alan Bond, along with his team at Reaction Engines, has

Magnetic Levitation

Even train engineers and designers are looking to the stars. James Powell, who invented magnetic levitation (maglev) trains, is using the same type of engineering to design a system to launch spaceships off of Earth. Instead of using a rocket, the spaceship would accelerate at high speeds above a set of magnetic tracks encased in a vacuum tube. While all the technology for this exists, building it on such a massive scale could take more than twenty years.

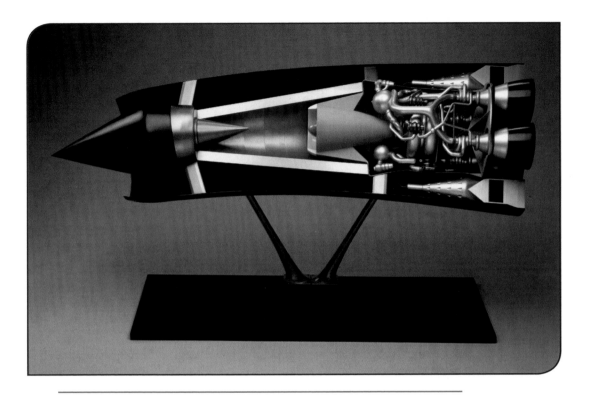

SABRE is designed to pull oxygen from the air to cut down on the amount of liquid oxygen that most spacecraft need to carry. That will make spacecraft lighter, which will allow them to travel faster.

developed an engine called SABRE (Synergistic Air Breathing Rocket Engine.) It works something like a supersonic jet engine. Instead of having to store large quantities of liquid oxygen to ignite the fuel, it takes oxygen out of the air to mix with the fuel to create thrust. This makes the spaceship lighter and works for the first stage after liftoff, or for as long as oxygen is available.

NASA is currently testing its newest Space Launch System (SLS). The SLS is a mega-rocket, the largest and most powerful rocket the

United States has ever built. It's designed to launch spacecraft beyond Earth orbit to asteroids and, eventually, to other planets.

Touchdown

It's one thing to launch spaceships off Earth. But returning them from space and making them land safely has its own set of engineering challenges.

Gravity serves as a force to pull a spaceship back to Earth. But the closer it gets to the surface, the faster it accelerates. One thing that slows it down is Earth's atmosphere. Particles in the atmosphere rub against the spacecraft, causing friction, which slows the speed of reentry. But friction also causes intense heat, as much as 3,000 degrees Fahrenheit (1,649 degrees Celsius). Without the proper design, the spaceship would burn up as it flies through the atmosphere.

Engineers have learned that designing a ship with a blunt-shaped surface creates a shock wave in front of the spaceship that keeps the heat at a distance. It also helps slow the ship down.

For added protection, engineers have designed different types of heat shields, along with insulation. The shields used on the Apollo command modules were made from an epoxy resin and fiberglass, which burned away from the spacecraft's surface, taking the heat with it. From the ground, it might have looked like the command module was on fire.

Tile grids were added to the underside of the space shuttle to absorb most of the heat. They were made of silica, the main component of sand. Some of the plates were made with carbon fibers, which are heat resistant. But the tiles broke easily, and there were many problems with them coming off the space shuttle upon reentry.

A similar shield to the one used in the Apollo missions, with an additional layer of metallic-based thermal coating, is being designed for the *Orion* ship that NASA plans to send to the moon.

The *Gemini 2* spacecraft sustained damage to its heat shield
when it entered Earth's atmosphere.

NASA is considering another option, an inflatable shield made of
fibers and fabrics that are heat resistant. It would be light, fold up into
a small space, and inflate when the spaceship goes through reentry.

Landing command modules safely after reentry is another problem
that engineers have had to solve. For most of the space program,
command modules used parachutes to slow them down until they
splashed down in the ocean.

The *Soyuz* module still uses parachutes but lands in the desert.
Just minutes before it lands, retro rockets fire from the bottom of the
command module, slowing it down even more.

Grasshopper Reusable Launch System

Not only is it economical to reuse spacecraft, but engineers knew it would also cost less if the rockets used to launch them were also reusable. In 2012, a company named SpaceX, founded by Elon Musk, began testing a reusable launch system called Grasshopper VTVL (vertical takeoff vertical landing.) Traditional rocket boosters burn up as they reenter Earth's atmosphere, but the Grasshopper does not. It also lands back in the exact same spot from where it took off.

For the *Curiosity* rover to land safely on Mars, engineers designed a new landing system called Sky Crane, which uses a tether as well as retro rockets to make a "soft landing."

Even though the space shuttle changed the way spaceships landed, by gliding back down like an airplane on a runway, most ships, like *Soyuz*, still return using command modules.

3

Speed, Shields, and Solar Sails

Once spaceships are launched into space, engineers face several more major questions:

- How will the ships keep moving?
- What materials should spaceships be made of?
- How will the hull and the astronauts be protected from space debris, meteorites, radiation, and extreme temperatures?
- What kind of interior space designs will accommodate astronauts, cargo, research tools, and life-support systems?

After reaching orbit, a spaceship needs propulsion to travel farther. Propulsion is what pushes an object forward. Even though technology has changed a great deal since the first rocket engines were made, the speed at which spaceships are able to travel has remained the same.

Ions

One method that is currently being used is ion propulsion. NASA has used ion propulsion technology for several decades. *Deep Space I*, a spacecraft used from 1998 to 2001, did flybys of asteroids and comets to collect data. It was the first to use the ion propulsion system. This type of system is different because it doesn't use liquid propellants, like *Voyager* and the Apollo spaceships. It uses electricity and gases like xenon to create thrust. However, it still doesn't travel as fast as scientists would like.

Eager to increase speeds, engineers are researching many different types of propulsion systems.

Solar Electric Propulsion (SEP)

A new form of ion propulsion is SEP, or solar electric propulsion, which will gather power from the sun by using solar panels that unfold after launch. Many of its components have been successfully tested at NASA's Glenn Research Center in Cleveland, Ohio. NASA expects to launch a vehicle within just a few years to demonstrate the use of SEP.

Plasma

Breakthroughs in plasma technology have been made by physicist and former astronaut Franklin Chang-Diaz. He calls his project VASIMR,

Solar Sails

Solar sails, which already exist, are another type of propulsion system that doesn't require a chemical propellant. Made of ultra-thin, aluminum-coated plastic, the sails are folded and wound around spools attached to flexible booms. The booms deploy after the spacecraft is in orbit, unfurling the sails. Light particles from the sun bounce off the surface of the sails and push it along. This continuing pressure causes the spacecraft to increase its speed over time. A nonprofit space organization, the Planetary Society, headed by Bill Nye ("the Science Guy") will soon launch its own solar sail-powered spacecraft, *LightSail 2*.

or Variable Specific Impulse Magnetoplasma Rocket. Plasma, made by stripping electrons away from fuel, is heated up by electricity. Magnetic fields then direct it to where it is ejected from the engine, creating thrust. One of the possible fuels for VASIMR is hydrogen, which can be found almost anywhere in the solar system. One possibility is that hydrogen could be collected as a spaceship travels to replenish the fuel instead of having to carry enough to reach the spaceship's destination.

Testing of plasma-propelled engines is in its early stages. Scientists use a vacuum chamber to test the VASIMR engine, designed by physicist and former astronaut Franklin Chang-Diaz.

Other options for the future include nuclear power and an electromagnetic drive (EMdrive.)

Nuclear Power

According to Sonny Mitchell, nuclear thermal propulsion project manager at NASA's Marshall Space Flight Center in Huntsville, Alabama, nuclear propulsion might be the best technology option to take spaceships to Mars and beyond. Designs are underway for these high-speed thrust engines, which are twice as efficient as those used for the space shuttles. But it will take a great deal more testing to ensure the safety of nuclear propulsion systems.

Electromagnetic (EM) Drive

The electromagnetic drive creates microwaves that bounce around inside a cone-shaped cavity. They push against one end of the cone, making the other, smaller end speed up in the opposite direction. There is no need to use a propellant. Many people believe EM drive will work, while others believe it's not possible. If it does eventually work, and work safely, it could provide the speed needed to reach another star system in a much shorter time than is now possible.

Protection

The fact that there is no atmosphere in space means there is no protection for a spaceship and its inhabitants and cargo. Radiation, mostly from the sun, as well as extreme temperatures, pose the biggest threats. In addition, ships need protection from space debris such as tiny meteor particles called micrometeorites.

To keep the ships' hulls intact and protect the crews, engineers have been tasked with deciding what kinds of materials spaceships should be made of. Titanium is one of the metals that has been

The universe is filled with all manner of space debris that can cause damage to spacecraft and their crew members.

used for spacecraft. It's very strong and lightweight and can handle extreme temperatures and pressure. Kevlar, like the material used in bulletproof vests, is another material that has been used for protective sheeting.

Mixtures of metals, called composites, have also been developed for use in space technology. Some are so small they can only be seen through special microscopes. Making composites at this extra-small level is called nanotechnology. Because of their structure, composites such as graphene and carbon nanotubes are extremely strong but still lightweight.

An insulating material called aerogel is used for protection from extreme temperatures. Aerogel, which means "frozen smoke," is made by taking all the liquid from a gel and replacing it with gas. This process makes aerogel like a sponge, filled with tiny pockets of air, which creates an effective heat insulator for spaceships.

A Whipple shield is another means used to protect spacecraft from space debris and micrometeorites. It's a type of bumper shield that acts like an umbrella to break up the particles as they hit the spaceship. Behind the shield are blankets made of ceramic cloth that break the particles up even more.

Robots

Robotics is an important aspect of designing spaceships. All of the probes and rovers that have traveled through space to explore the other planets in our solar system are basically giant robots. Robotic arms can perform repairs outside of the ship. Human-like robots, like Robonaut 2, can perform repetitive or dangerous tasks instead of the astronauts. They also don't need food or life support, sleep or spacesuits. They can work outside the ship as well as inside. They are not as likely to be harmed by the effects of radiation as humans are.

In order to keep from floating in the weightlessness of the ISS as they sleep, astronauts must use specially designed personal sleep stations.

Passengers

What about the astronauts, and someday, commercial passengers? Besides the protection on the outside from shields and insulation, engineers must also consider the interior of spaceships. Room has to be made for cargo, fuel, and research and repair tools, as well as life-support systems in very compact areas.

Because there is no gravity in space, weightlessness, not only of people but also of objects, is a unique problem facing engineers. Astronauts can't just lie down in a bed to go to sleep; they have to learn to sleep attached to something, such as the sleep pods on the International Space Station. They also need enough space to move around. Instruments, liquids, food, and cargo must all be kept contained.

It takes thousands of engineers and scientists, plus many years of research, to make sure that the spaceships they have designed and the cargo and astronauts that travel in them are safe and well protected from the dangers of space travel.

What's Up Next?

What progress has been made in the field of spaceship technology during the first two decades of the twenty-first century? In addition to new rocket launch, landing, and propulsion systems, engineers are planning new missions and science fiction–inspired spaceships to take us into the future.

Space Tourism

Several private companies have been testing suborbital ships to carry passengers into space for brief periods of time before returning them to Earth.

One of these ships is called *New Shepard* and is made by a company called Blue Origin. Its founder is Jeff Bezos, the owner of Amazon.com.

New Shepard will launch using the VTVL (vertical takeoff vertical landing) system. A pressurized capsule, which can hold up to six people, will sit atop the booster rocket. It will zoom into space for two and a half minutes, passing the Karman Line. The capsule will separate from the booster, coast into space, then return for a rocket-controlled vertical landing. The whole system can be reused.

A successful landing of Blue Origin's *New Shepard* suborbital spacecraft is proof that the VTVL system works. Ships like these will be used for space tourism.

Another suborbital plane, designed by Burt Rutan of Richard Branson's Virgin Galactic company, is called *SpaceShip Two*. Unlike *New Shepard*, it will launch from a "mother ship," *White Knight Two*, from 50,000 miles (80,467 km) up in the air. It will detach and fly from the mother ship to about 68 miles (110 km) into space. Up to six passengers, plus two pilots, will experience weightlessness for about four minutes before gliding back to Earth. The entire trip will last about two and a half hours.

Shuttles to the ISS

Three other private companies have contracted with NASA to build ships with the purpose of transporting cargo and, eventually, ferrying astronaut crews to and from the International Space Station.

One of them is called *Dream Chaser*. A product of Sierra Nevada Corporation, *Dream Chaser* looks like a giant manta ray with its fins pointing to the sky. Still in the testing stage, it can hold a crew of seven and should be reusable up to fifteen times or more.

Boeing's *CST-100 Starliner*, also still in testing stages, looks more like Apollo's cone-shaped command module. Plans include carrying

o—••••→ Elon Musk

The founder of SpaceX and creator of the Falcon 9 rocket, plus the *Dragon* spaceship, Elon Musk made history when *Dragon* became the first privately owned spacecraft to deliver supplies for the astronauts at the International Space Station. The Falcon 9 rocket has also launched several satellites into orbit, such as the Deep Space Climate Observatory. Musk is a famous businessman whose inventions and business ventures will have a long-lasting impact on the future of space travel and exploration.

The SpaceX *Dragon* is used to shuttle cargo back and forth to the International Space Station.

four-man crews, plus cargo and scientific research materials, to the ISS. Boeing projects that it can reuse *Starliner* about ten times.

The only one of these spaceships that has already delivered cargo to the ISS is called *Dragon*. It is the product of a company called Space Exploration Technologies Corporation, or SpaceX. *Dragon* first docked with the ISS on May 25, 2012, and has made many successful trips since. It is launched vertically, using the SpaceX-designed Falcon 9 rocket system. After leaving Earth's atmosphere, giant solar panels unfold to harness energy from the sun.

Dragon is also designed to accommodate an astronaut crew of up to seven astronauts as well as cargo. That version will be the same size but will be called *Dragon 2*. In addition, it has a research component called DragonLab, which will be used to conduct experiments while in orbit, where there is very little gravity, without having to use the ISS. It's also part of a plan to take passengers for a ride around the moon.

New Missions to the Moon

Why go back to the moon?

Some private companies look to the moon as a new source to mine mineral resources. NASA sees it as a testing ground for new technologies and spaceships, like its newest one, *Orion*.

Orion will use the Space Launch System (SLS) to carry out a mission called Exploration Mission-1, or EM-1. The unmanned mission will last twenty-five days and make a large orbit around the moon. EM-2 will carry a crew of astronauts.

Orion has three parts: the service module, the crew module, and the Launch Abort System (LAS.) The service module, designed by the European Space Agency, will hold the power and propulsion system. On the outside, solar panels will collect sunlight to create electricity. The middle section will hold the crew, while the LAS is designed to detach and carry the crew to safety in case of an emergency.

The unmanned spacecraft *Orion* reached an altitude of 3,600 miles (5,794 km) above Earth and completed two full orbits.

CubeSats

CubeSats are lightweight, cube-shaped satellites, only 4 inches (10 centimeters) on each side, but powerhouses when it comes to collecting scientific data. Thirteen of them will travel with NASA's EM-1 mission and will be deployed to gather data from the moon. NASA hopes to learn more about soil conditions, landing sites, water sources, and more. Skyfire, a CubeSat made by Lockheed Martin, uses infrared technology. Scientists expect CubeSats to make a big impact on space missions. They will collect data that will help engineers decide which materials and designs will make space travel safer and more efficient.

NASA also plans to build a spaceport somewhere between Earth and the moon called Deep Space Gateway (DSG). The spaceport will serve as a place from which to launch missions to the moon's surface, as well as a gateway to other planets in the solar system. Built to be used by many countries besides the United States, it will be assembled in space and powered by solar electric propulsion.

Along with the spaceport, NASA is planning to build Deep Space Transport (DST), a 41-ton (37 metric tons) spaceship that would leave from Deep Space Gateway for missions to Mars and, eventually, to other planets. It would be reusable and provide living space for astronauts as they traveled, then return them to the DSG.

Plans for the Gateway and the DST will span the 2020s. NASA is also considering manning a yearlong flight of the DST around the moon to test its readiness to transport a crew to Mars.

Where No One Has Gone Before

Many space technologies at the beginning of the twenty-first century have focused on the ISS, new fuel systems, and plans for the moon missions. Even more exciting, dreams of finally landing a manned spaceship on the planet Mars are coming closer and closer to becoming reality.

Voyage to Mars

The engineers at NASA are channeling many of their efforts in this direction. They have mapped out a three-part plan for the future Mars missions.

The first part, called Earth Reliant, focuses on research aboard the ISS from now through the mid 2020s. It will test and develop new technologies, communications, and systems for human health and protection during deep space travel.

The second section, Proving Ground, will be conducted from 2018 through 2030. All the activities planned near the moon and with the Deep Space Gateway will prepare astronauts for the voyages to Mars and other planets. NASA's Asteroid Redirect Mission will send a robotic spacecraft to retrieve an asteroid from space and place it in orbit around the moon. Astronauts will gather samples from the asteroid and practice spacewalking in preparation for Mars missions.

The final part, Earth Independent, is already in process. Probes and land rovers have been transmitting information from Mars to prepare spaceships for landing and finding possible areas for astronauts to live. Finally, in the early part of the 2030s, astronauts will travel to Mars.

Other countries, as well as some private companies and organizations, also have plans to journey to Mars.

China has emerged in the twenty-first century as a new space superpower. Its engineers have successfully established an orbiting space station, launched a spaceship to the moon, and plan to have bases on the moon and Mars by the middle of the century.

A Dutch nonprofit company called Mars One plans to establish a permanent human colony on Mars, beginning with a crew of four, in 2023. Several unmanned flights will precede the manned spacecraft to prepare the colony for habitation.

Mars Direct, a project by scientist Robert Zubrin, plans to launch an Earth Return Vehicle directly to Mars from Earth. It would deliver components to create rocket propellants using carbon dioxide from

Mars Rover 2020

The newest Mars Rover will launch in mid-2020 and land on the Red Planet in February 2021. It will give scientists even more information to prepare for the eventual landing of spaceships and their crews on Mars. The rover will test landing techniques, identify sources of subsurface water, and test methods for producing oxygen from the atmosphere. It will also analyze weather conditions that will affect the way future astronauts will live and work on the planet's surface.

Probes and rovers are scouting the conditions on Mars in preparation for future missions to the Red Planet.

the atmosphere on Mars. Two years later, a crew, along with a Mars Habitat Unit, would arrive to explore the planet for eighteen months. They would return using the fuel that was produced on the planet from the first mission.

A similar program, called Project Troy, has been proposed by Reaction Engines, Ltd. All plans provide a way to make fuel on Mars for a return trip, along with habitats for the crews.

Visions of the Future

What are the plans for future space exploration? What new kinds of spaceships are being imagined and planned for?

One of those plans is called Breakthrough Starshot and is the brainchild of famous astrophysicist Stephen Hawking and Russian billionaire Yuri Milner. If realized, the project will launch thousands of nanocrafts, tiny robotic spacecrafts equipped with solar sails, to "fly" through space to Alpha Centauri, the closest star system to ours. Its mission will be to discover whether Alpha Centauri contains an Earth-like planet.

This "StarChip" is designed to gather data from the Alpha Centauri star system. The solar sail–propelled nanocraft will fly through space in search of life-sustaining planets in the Alpha Centauri system.

The nanocrafts will be lightweight and look like a cell-phone chip with a thin solar sail. They will carry cameras and communication equipment. Light beams will propel the ships, which are expected to reach 20 percent the speed of light. At that speed, the nanocrafts could possibly reach Alpha Centauri in about twenty years. Information would reach Earth about four years later. With the spaceships we have now, it would take thirty thousand years to reach Alpha Centauri, which is 25 trillion miles (40.2 trillion km) away.

Though the research portion of Breakthrough Starshot will take a number of years, if it's successful, discovering if there is life similar to ours in another star system could happen in just a few decades.

Engineers are designing spaceships that we may not see until many years into the future. One of these, the Bussard funnel, would use an enormous magnetic funnel to collect hydrogen for fuel, eliminating the need to carry fuel on the spaceship. However, the funnel is so large, engineers think it might cause too much drag for the ship to keep moving.

Another concept developed by a NASA team is the Nautilus X. It uses current technology and is designed to travel through space. Though unable to land on other planets, it could serve as a docking station for landing spaceships. It would be solar-powered and provide space farms to grow food for the astronauts.

The Skylon spaceplane, invented by Alan Bond, uses the SABRE rocket engine plus a horizontal takeoff and landing system. Resembling a sleek, black torpedo, it will be completely reusable and need minimal repairs. Bond's intention is to replace standard rocket-

Space Exploration Vehicle

NASA has built the model for a vehicle that would not only be used to collect data as it travels across a planet's or asteroid's surface, but would also be part of the spaceship itself. It's called the Space Exploration Vehicle, or SEV, and will include manipulator arms to handle satellites and other objects in space. About the same size as a pickup truck, the SEV will be able to easily maneuver a planet's surface. With twelve wheels, it can climb over rocks and move sideways like a crab.

launch systems. He told Space TV Network, SEN, "If we manage to pull this off, then by the time we get to 2030, access to space will be more like you see in science fiction films than the way it is today. So, regular vehicles flying into orbit and back again on a daily basis... That will actually be with us and that is something pretty exciting to look forward to."

Stephen Hawking views the twenty-first century as a new space age, one that needs a new generation of explorers to venture into space and change the world for good. Who will these explorers be? They will be the kids of today who love math and science, computers and puzzles, sci-fi books and movies. The inventors. The planners. The dreamers. The future engineers. They will take us not just to Mars, but also to the edge of the solar system and possibly even beyond.

CHRONOLOGY

1926

Robert Goddard invents liquid-propellant rocket engine.

1962

John Glenn orbits Earth.

1969

The *Apollo 11* lands on the moon on July 20; Neil Armstrong walks on the moon on July 21.

1981

On April 12, the first reusable spaceship, the space shuttle, is launched.

2000

First crew boards the International Space Station on November 2.

2004

Rovers *Spirit* and *Opportunity* land on the surface of Mars.

2012

Voyager 1 probe leaves our solar system and crosses into interstellar space.

2018

NASA plans to launch unmanned *Orion* spacecraft into an orbit around the moon.

2020–2029

NASA will establish Deep Space Gateway, an outpost near the moon.

2031–2038

The United States and Russia will send manned expeditions to Mars.

BIBLIOGRAPHY

Allison, Peter Ray. "What Will Power Tomorrow's Spaceships?" BBC, January 20, 2016. Retrieved August 20, 2017. http://www.bbc.com/future/story/20160119-what-will-power-tomorrows-spacecraft.

Boeing. "Beyond Earth: Path to Mars." Retrieved September 1, 2017. http://beyondearth.com/path-to-mars.

Dodson, Brian. "StarTram—Maglev Train to Low Earth Orbit." New Atlas, March 9, 2012. http://www.newatlas.com/startram-maglev-to-leo/21700.

Electronic Products. "Top 10 Engineering Advancements of 21st Century." March 14, 2014. http://www.electronicproducts.com/Electromechanical_Components/Electromechanical_Switches/Top_10_engineering_advancements_of_21st_century.aspx.

Miller, Ron. *Spaceships: An Illustrated History of the Real and the Imagined.* Washington, DC: Smithsonian Books, 2016.

NASA. "Journey to Mars." Retrieved September 8, 2017. http://www.nasa.gov/content/journey-to-mars-overview.

NASA. "Orion Spacecraft." Retrieved August 21, 2017. http://www.nasa.gov/exploration/systems/orion/index.html.

NASA. "What Is the Soyuz Spacecraft?" July 30, 2013. http://www.nasa.gov/audience/forstudents/5-8/features/nasa-knows/what-is-the-soyuz-spacecraft-58.

Shubber, Kadhim. "Skylon: Alan Bond's Mission to Replace Space Rockets with Spaceplanes." *Wired*, August 12, 2013. www.wired.co.uk/article/skylon-alan-bond.

Skocik, Collin. "VASIMR Plasma Engine: Earth to Mars in 39 Days?" Spaceflight Insider, July 19, 2017. http://www.spaceflightinsider.com/conferences/humans-to-mars/vasimr-plasma-engine-earth-mars-39-days.

Space X. "Dragon." Retrieved September 1. http://www.spacex.com/dragon.

Virgin Atlantic. "These Are the Vehicles That Will Take You to Space." Retrieved September 1, 2017. http://www.virgingalactic.com/human-spaceflight/our-vehicles.

Wall, Mike. "Mars Samples May Come to Earth via NASA's Deep Space Gateway." Space.com. Retrieved September 1, 2017. http://www.space.com/37154-nasa-deep-space-gateway-mars-samples.html.

Woollaston, Victoria, and Ellie Zolfagharifard. "Take Us to the Stars: Stephen Hawking and Mark Zuckerberg Launch $100m Alien-hunting Mission with Russian Billionaire to Send Feet of Nano-craft to Alpha Centauri at 20% of the Speed of Light." Daily Mail, April 12, 2016. www.dailymail.co.uk/sciencetech/article-3536191/Stephen-Hawking-Yuri-Milner-Mark-Zuckerberg-reveal-100m-Starshot-alien-hunting-mission-using-light-propelled-starship-travel-Alpha-Centauri.html.

aerogel A material in which most of the liquid has been replaced by pockets of air.

gravity The force that attracts an object to Earth.

ion An atom that carries a positive or negative electrical charge.

Karman Line An imaginary line that is 62 miles (100 km) above Earth, where the atmosphere ends and outer space begins.

launch To send or shoot into the air.

magnetic levitation A system that suspends and propels an object above a surface at high speeds using magnetism.

micrometeorite A very small particle in outer space.

nanotechnology Science and engineering on a microscopic scale.

plasma Matter that has been subjected to an electromagnetic charge.

propulsion A force that pushes something forward.

robot A computerized machine that carries out complex tasks.

space debris Objects that are in orbit or floating in space.

space probe A spacecraft designed to travel through space to record and transmit data.

suborbital Flying beyond Earth's atmosphere but not reaching orbit.

suspended animation A slowing of a body's life processes without the body dying.

FURTHER READING

Books

Aldrin, Buzz, and Marianne J. Dyson. *Welcome to Mars: Making a Home on the Red Planet.* Washington, DC: National Geographic, 2015.

Furgang, Kathy. *Rocket Science and Spacecraft Fundamentals.* New York, NY: Britannica Educational Publishing/Rosen Publishing Group, 2018.

Reyes, Ray. *STEAM Jobs in Space Exploration* (STEAM Jobs You'll Love). Vero Beach, FL: Rourke Publishing Group, 2017.

Richmond, Benjamin. *Life in Space: Beyond Planet Earth.* New York, NY: Sterling Children's Books, 2018.

Websites

ESA Kids, the European Space Agency

www.esa.int/esaKIDSen/index.html

Website of the European Space Agency, where kids can learn all about space and space programs.

NASA Kids' Club

www.nasa.gov/kidsclub/index.html

An interactive website about NASA for kids that includes games, fun facts, and information.

Popular Science: Space

www.popsci.com/space

A site with current information about the newest things that are happening in space science.

INDEX